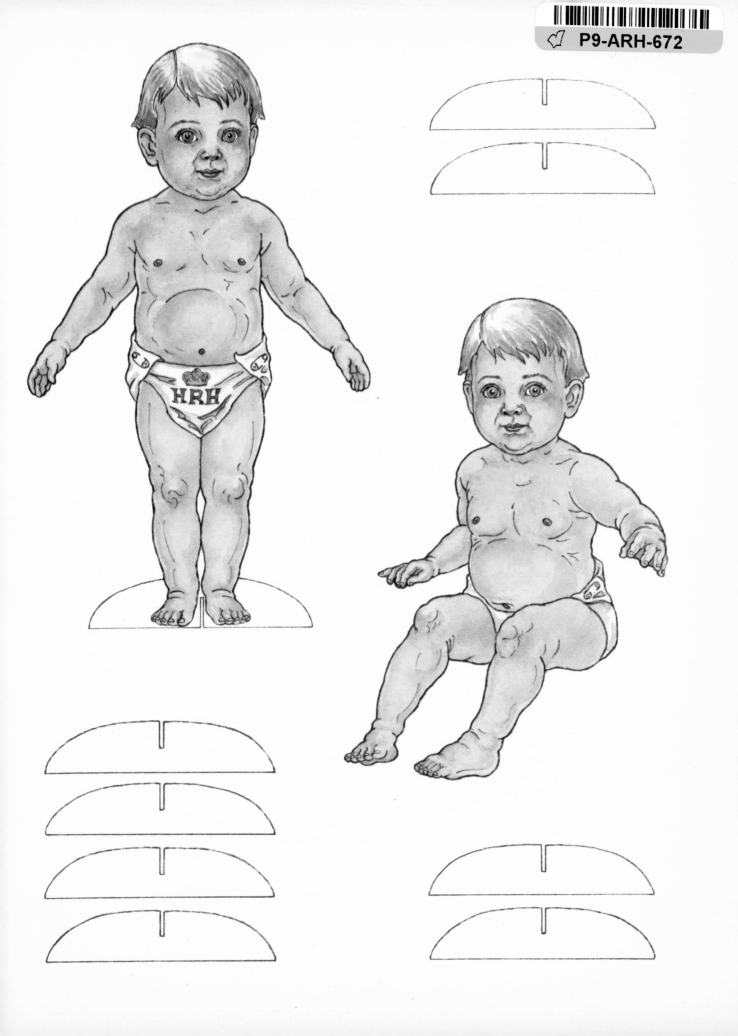

The Royal Baby
THE PRIVATE LIFE OF HIS ROYAL HIGHNESS
P·R·I·N·C·E W·I·L·L·I·A·M

A PAPER DOLL BOOK
By Clarissa Harlowe and Cathy Camhy
Design: Sara Giovanitti · Illustration: Emanuel Schongut

Another Original Publication of Pocket Books

POCKET BOOKS
A Division of Simon & Schuster, Inc.
1230 Avenue of the Americas, New York, N.Y. 10020

•

Text Copyright © 1983 by Rollene W. Saal Associates
Illustrations copyright © 1983 by Emanuel Schongut
Designed by Sara Giovanitti

For information address
Pocket Books,
1230 Avenue of the Americas, New York, N.Y. 10020

ISBN: 0-671-49892-4

First Pocket Books printing November, 1983

10 9 8 7 6 5 4 3 2 1

P·R·I·N·C·E W·I·L·L·I·A·M

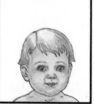

Prince William of Wales, firstborn of Prince Charles and Princess Diana, is second in line to the British throne. He will one day become William V, King of England. There have been only two previous Williams of any note, and both were foreigners: William of Normandy, who conquered England in 1066, and William of Orange, a 17th-century Dutchman who married into the Royal family.

This William is all English—except for a few branches on the family trees which connect him to such personages as Ghenghis Khan (on Dad's side) and Humphrey Bogart (on Mum's). He's got the common touch—having been born (on June 21, 1982) in a quite ordinary hospital, and has a sturdy constitution—he went home (to a quite *un*ordinary palace) when he was only one day old.

He made his official debut at his christening on August 4, swathed in an 1841 silk and lace christening gown—a hand-me-down from Great-great-great-Grandfather Edward VII. At the gilt baptismal font, the Archbishop of Canterbury intoned traditional prayers, as no fewer than six godparents—including a king, a commoner, a lord, a princess, a lady and a duchess—stood in proud attendance. They, and about 2,000 other admirers, gave him presents. There were hymns and holy water, cake and champagne. Young "Wills"—as his parents call him—dozed during the festivities.

He is already a seasoned traveler, having journeyed "Down Under" to Australia and New Zealand with his parents and his nanny, Miss Barnes, when he was not yet a year old. It was there that he held his very first press conference: dressed in jaunty apricot rompers, he did a fast barefoot crawl, showed both his teeth in a winning smile, and may or may not have said "Dada."

Prince William learned early on that being born to the purple has its duties as well as its privileges: he was the sole host at his first birthday party—attended by some wee royal cousins. Mum and Dad were away on an official tour of Canada and had to miss the celebration—but they called him long distance each day.

This winning chap with the long name (William Arthur Philip Louis) has made an auspicious start to a long and prosperous reign as first in the hearts of his countrymen—and people of good will the world over.

My grandma, the Queen, says that it is never too early to take our Royal Duty seriously.

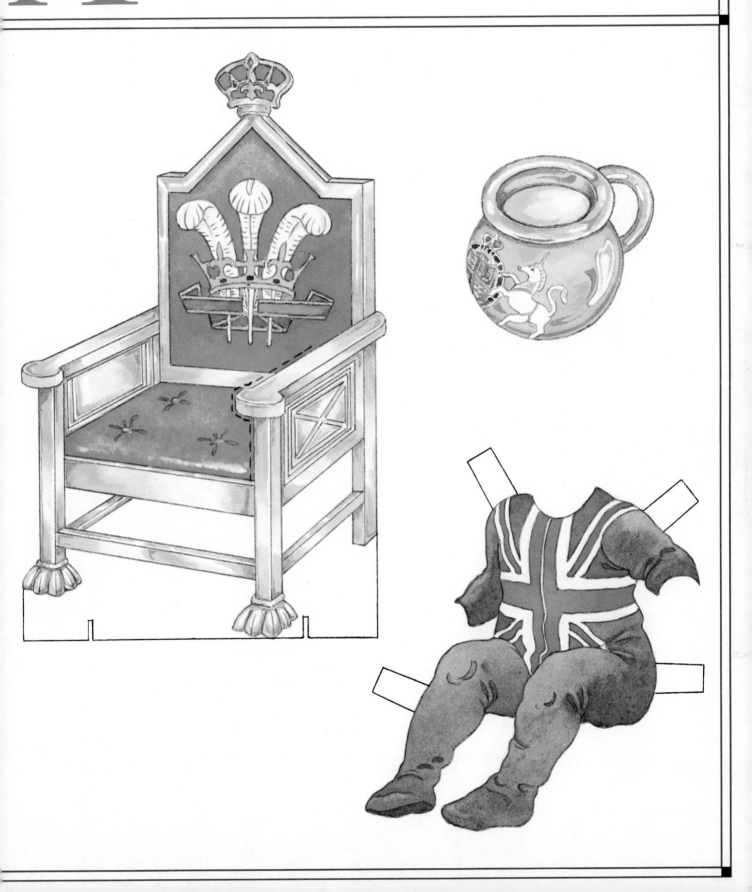

For our morning outing with Nanny Barnes, We like the informality of a Prince of Wales plaid suit.

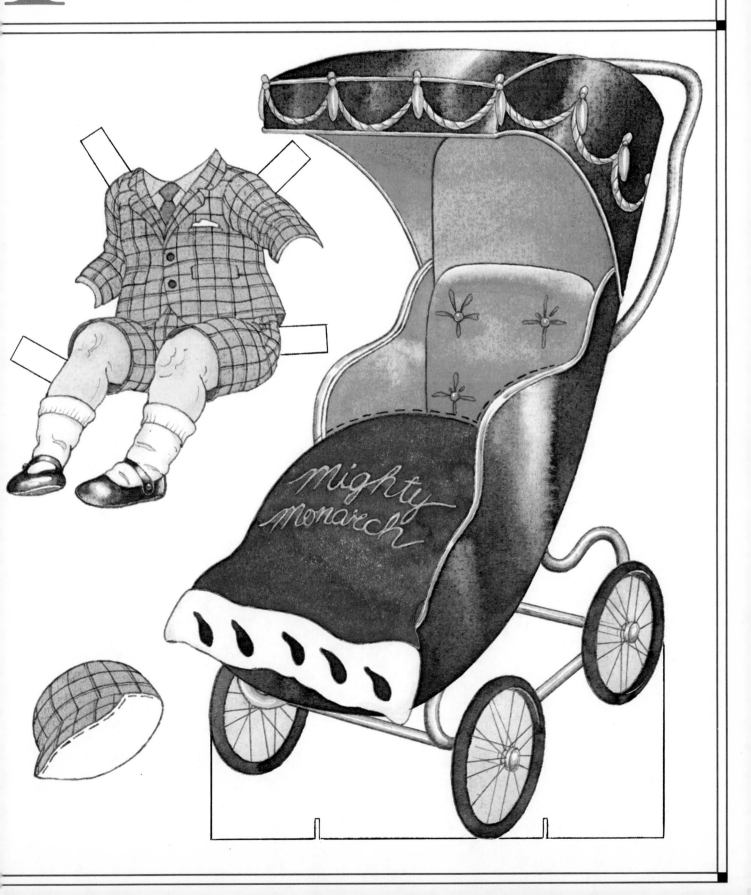

Someday I'll be Commander of the Royal Guards, but for now, it's jolly good wearing a bearskin hat.

T
he Empire was not built upon shifting sands, so today
We shall build ourselves a new castle.

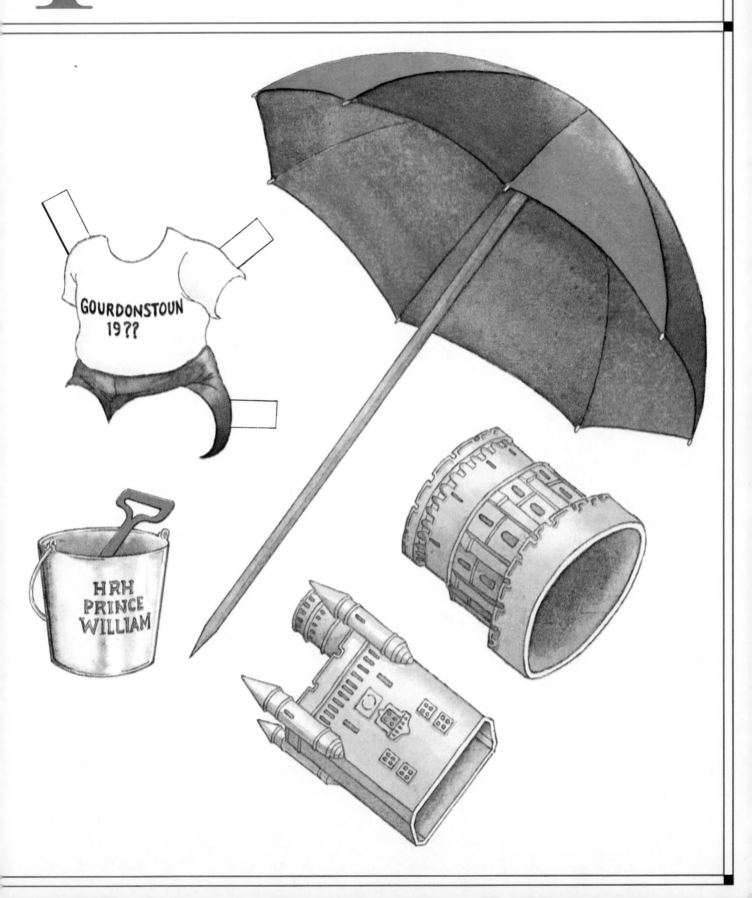

D

on't We look smashing in our Ascot gear? Our Shetland pony will accompany us on a "walkabout."

K

ippers and kidneys are all very well...but, at the moment,
We are partial to Yorkshire pudd.

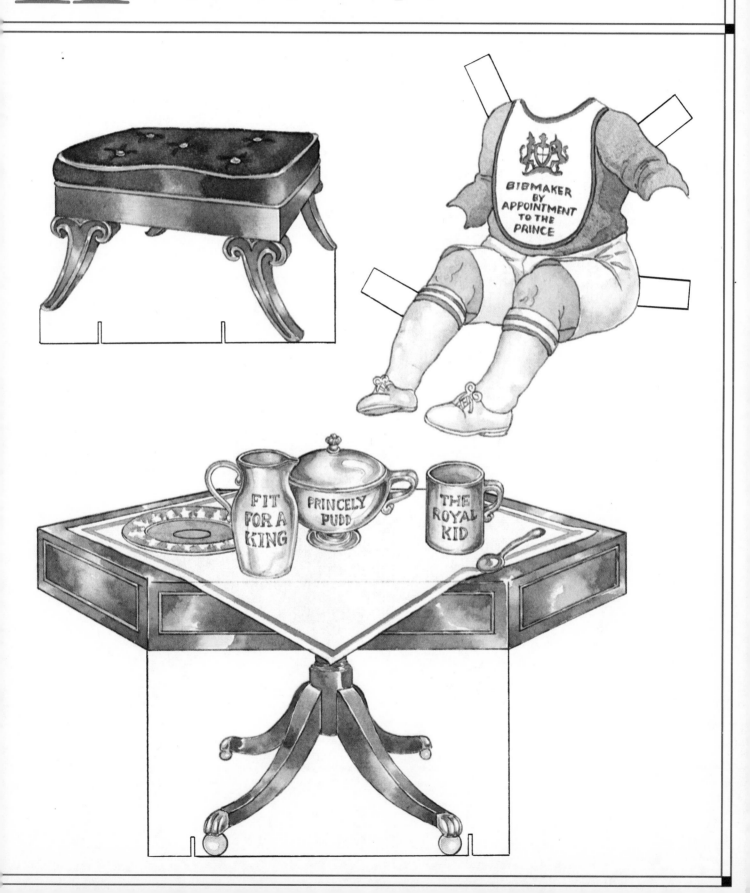

Fishing at Balmoral with my great-granny, the Queen Mum, is simply super. Look what We have caught!

On a fine English day, William goes out to play in the palace gardens. Sometimes his young friends, Lord Freddy Windsor and his sister Lady Gabriella, come over with their nannies. Daddy's faithful labrador, Harvey, makes sure that the royal kids don't stray. He never never splashes in the princely wading pool or digs a hole in William's sandbox. Harvey is content merely to serve as the loyal guardian of our little Prince.

ncle Andy gave me my helicopter suit, but I often get nabbed for speeding down the palace halls.

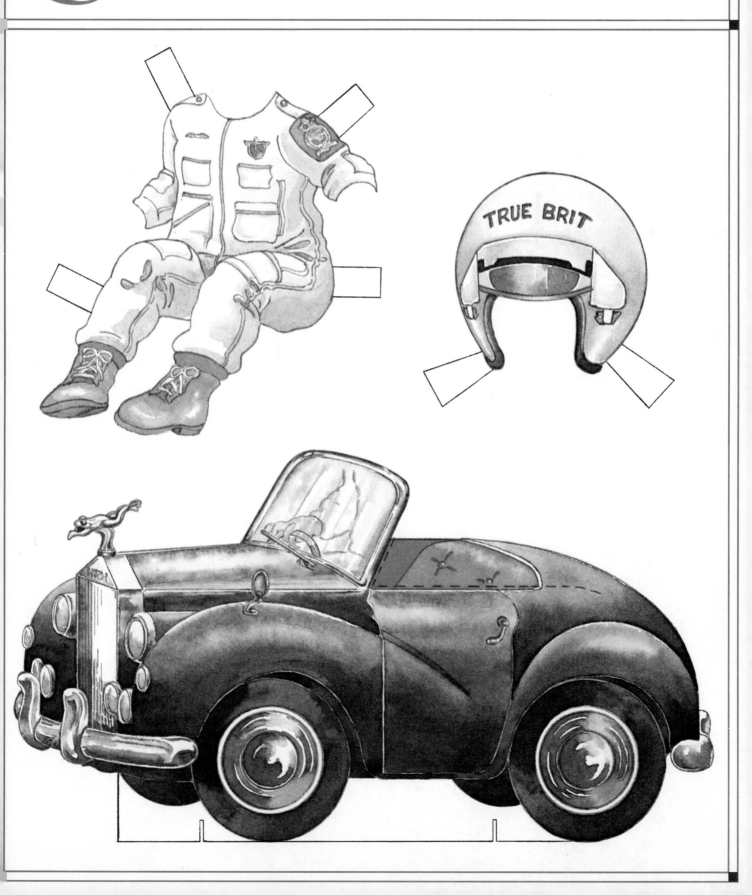

M

ummy loathes blood sports, but Daddy knows what's good for men...and future kings like him and me.

We are never too young to go down to the sea in ships, says William, ready to sail forth before the Royal mast.

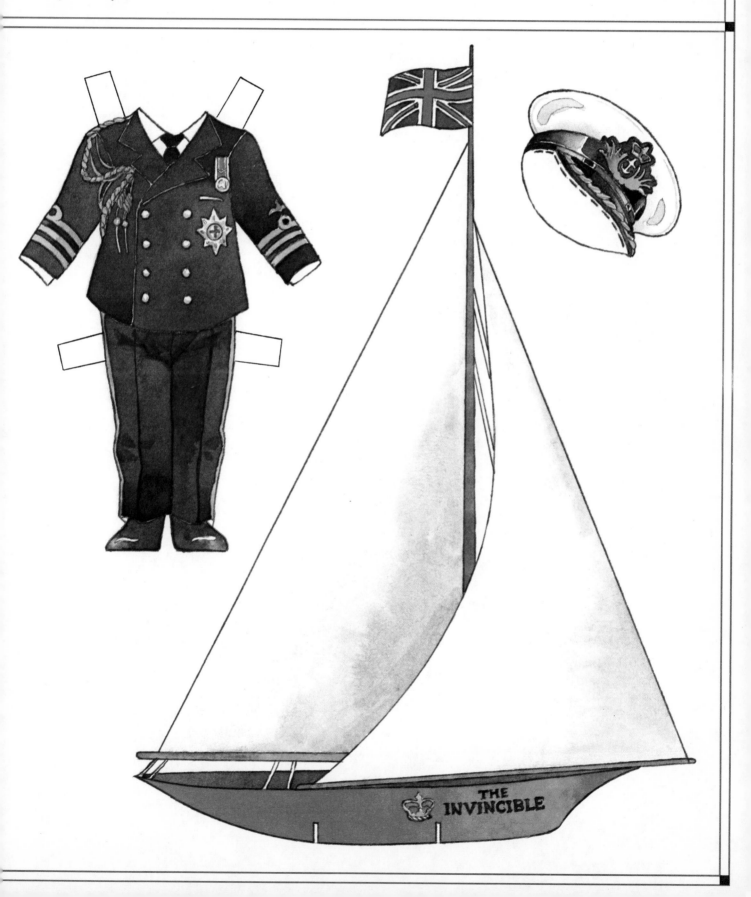

THE INVINCIBLE

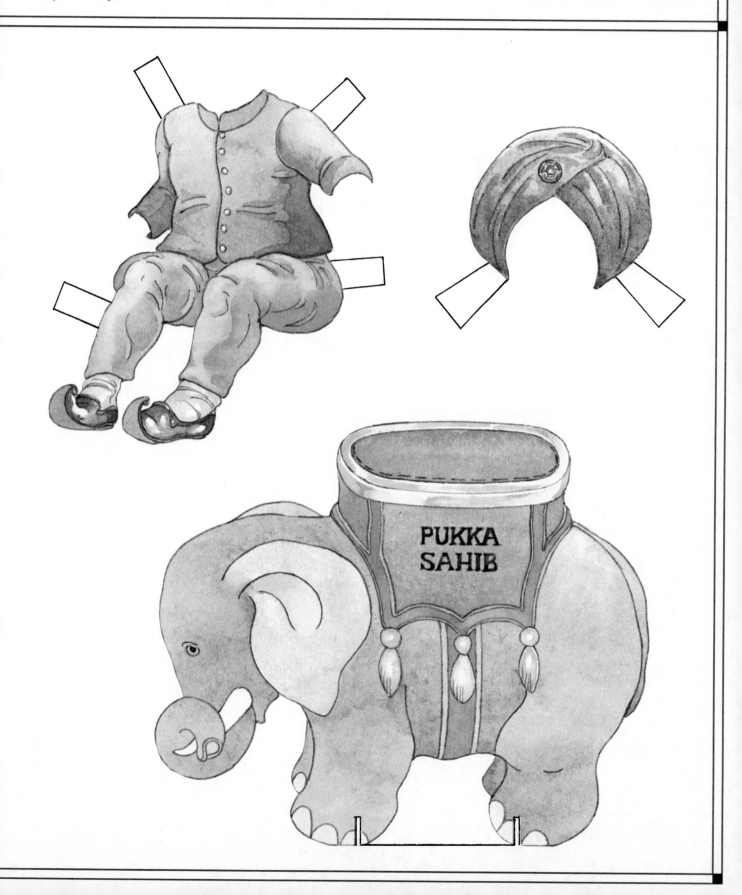

PUKKA
SAHIB

We to recall those glorious days when the sun
never set on the British Empire. Elephants and tigers

PUMA

W

e Royals sometimes go down, down into the mines, just the way our loyal subjects do.

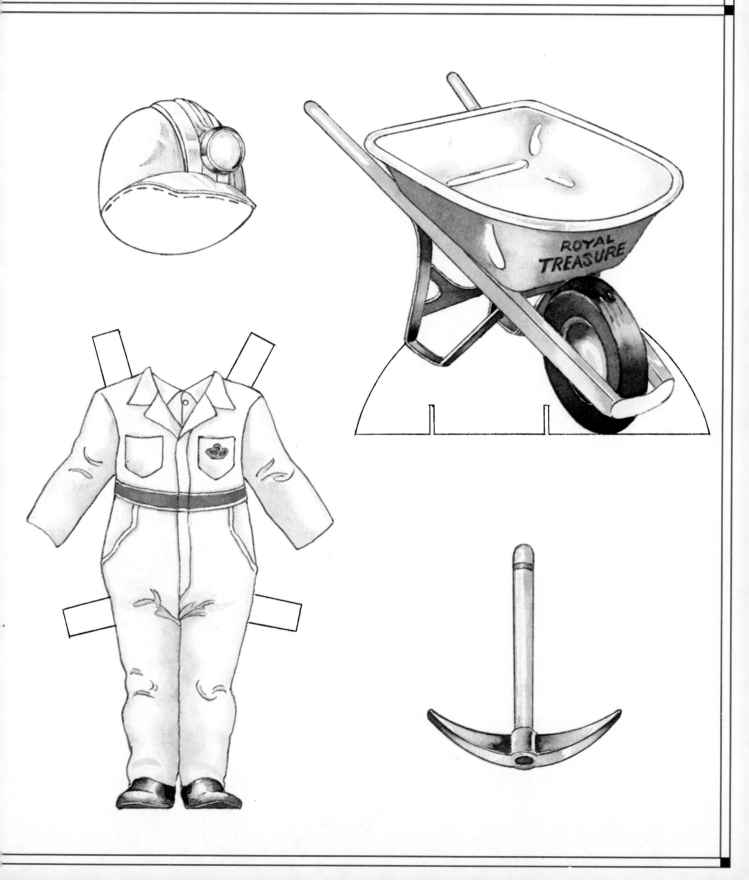

Queen Victoria loved the kilt...and so do We. Bet you can't guess what I wear beneath mine.

Daddy is good at polo. Grandpa Philip was better, but We are going to be the best ever.

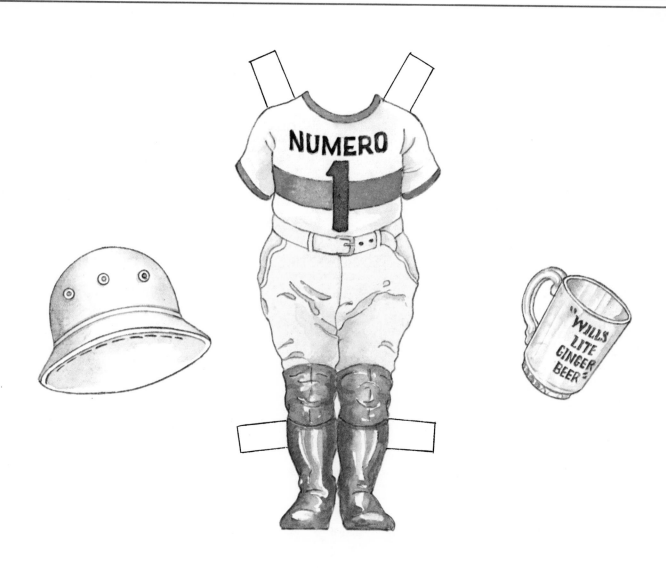

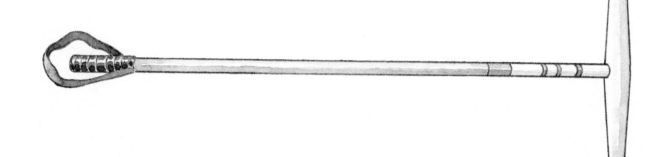

Good night all. Trust me: There will always be an England. Rule Britannia.

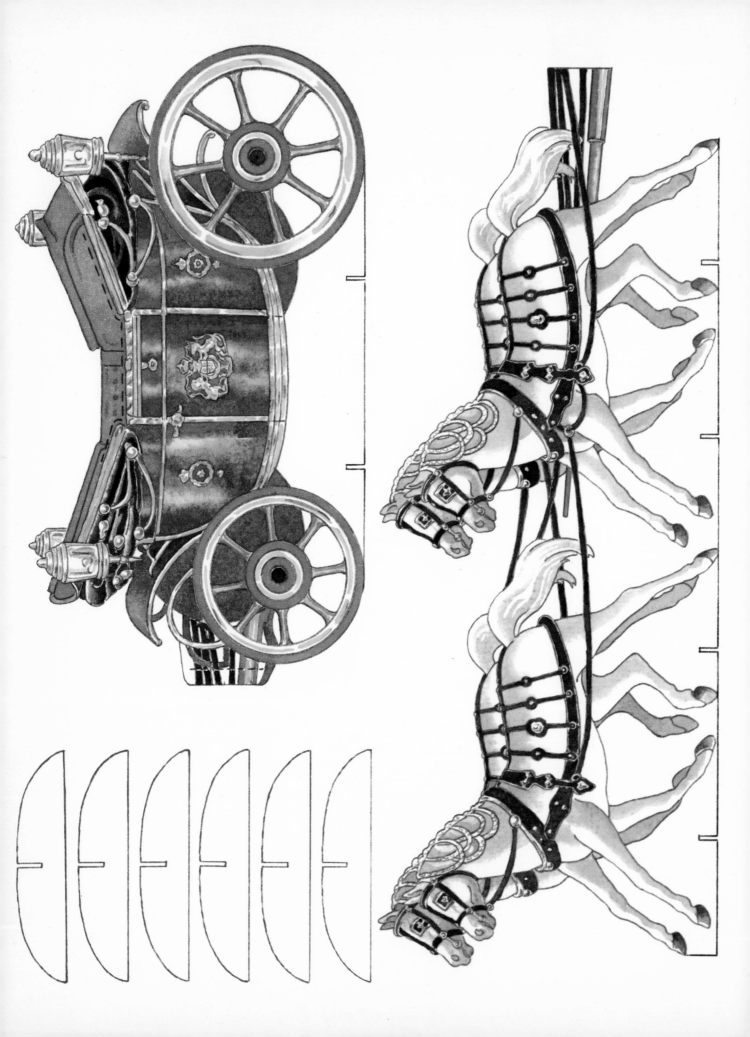